A Piece of Silver

✴ A Story of Christ ✴

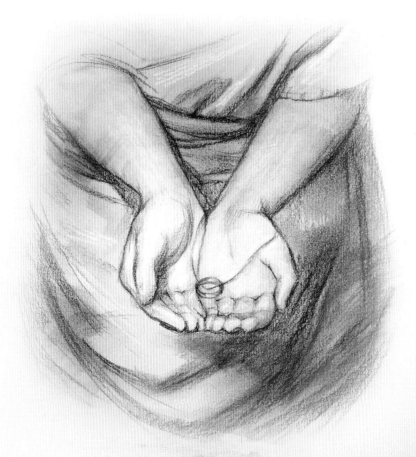

Clark Rich Burbidge

Illustrated by Annie Henrie Nader

For more information visit: www.apieceofsilver.com

Text © 2023 Clark Rich Burbidge
Illustrations © 2023 Annie Henrie Nader
All rights reserved.

ISBN 13: 978-1-4621-4616-1
ISBN 13: 978-1-4621-3148-8 (ebook)

Published by CFI, an imprint of Cedar Fort, Inc.
2373 W. 700 S., Suite 100, Springville, UT 84663
Distributed by Cedar Fort, Inc., www.cedarfort.com

Library of Congress Control Number: 2023938855

Printed in China

10 9 8 7 6 5 4 3 2 1

Printed on acid-free paper

A Piece of Silver

✳ *A Story of Christ* ✳

For my eleven grandchildren . . .

. . . and all those other
angels yet to grace our
presence.

A homeless boy wandered the alleys and back-ways of Bethlehem. His name was Daniel Ben-Yosef, but that name was not known to any living person. Those who crossed his path, and thought to address him at all, simply called him boy.

He had no hope, for his life stretched before him only as far as the next moment, and his dreams could not see beyond the next meal. How this forgotten child had survived to the tender age of eleven, no one knew, but then no one really noticed him anyway. He had no home, but was bright and resourceful and managed to find some corner to curl up in at the end of each day.

Only one possession could be called his own. It was nothing really, a small trinket. A ring he was given by his mother as she lay dying one late evening by the roadside. They had hoped for a better life in a new town, but the nights were cold on the long walk from Samaria and his mother, frail and worn down by life, could endure no more.

The ring was a simple silver ornament that hung around his neck, held there by a piece of twine. It was his only tie to the mother he loved and tried to remember every day. He did his best to honor his mother's wishes to live an honest life by finding whatever work was available for the untrained outsider. But Bethlehem was a difficult place for a poor young stranger to make his way. Each day was much the same as the next, little changed, until that one unusual night.

He lay curled up with mules and goats in the coarse straw of a stable behind an inn where he had occasionally found work sweeping and cleaning up. He had been asked to clean out the stables once and, as he kept a keen eye out for possible sleeping areas, felt at the time that the warm stable might make a nice bed if needed. It was quiet, and Daniel was drifting back to happier times with his mother when he realized he was not alone. He heard noises and hushed voices from the neighboring stall and feared at first that it might be the innkeeper, and that he might get in trouble since he had not asked permission to bed down in the stable.

At first, he lay as still as the straw around him, but at length a young boy's curiosity won out. Carefully, he glanced through a small crack in the wall. A young couple seemed to be settling down for the night in the neighboring stall. The woman appeared very uncomfortable, and the man looked like he had borne the weight of the world and failed in all that mattered, finding only a pile of straw to comfort his ailing wife in her time of need. Realizing it was not the innkeeper, the boy peeked over the rail and saw that the woman was in real difficulty for she was about to give birth. Daniel felt ashamed that he was watching such a personal moment. He burrowed deep into the straw with eyes tightly shut and hands pressed to his ears as if to say to himself, "I am not here." But he was there, and he heard her pained cries grow with each passing moment until it was impossible to sleep.

Suddenly, the woman was silent and a new sound was heard; the sound of a newborn gasping for its first breath and testing its lungs. This drew him out of his burrow and back to the edge of the rail for another look. Maybe a little bit longer look this time, he thought. He had never seen a baby this new before. It was so small, and its hands were tiny as they held the father's finger. The animals in the stable seemed strangely silent, almost reverent. Daniel felt something different in the air too; something wonderful and familiar.

He looked again at the young family and caught the mother's eye and smiled uneasily. She smiled back, and the young father followed her gaze to Daniel. At first the boy was afraid, but was comforted as the young father said, "Peace be with you my young friend, tonight is born to you a Savior, who is Christ the Lord." The young boy understood not the words, but felt a burning in his heart that he would always remember.

They were all silent for a while, resting. Then, through the window, the young boy noticed a most unusual star that seemed to shine down only on the humble stable. He heard beautiful music and singing echoing across the countryside. It was different than the music of the Bazaar, and the voices gave hope and comfort to his heart.

S oon they were not alone. Others came; mostly shepherds. A few he recognized, for he had occasionally obtained work in the fields. They knelt and gave thanks for something called a Messiah. This was something special, he could tell, but what it meant he did not understand.

He knelt there for some time, quietly watching from his neighboring stall. Others came and went; some praised God and called the newborn Emmanuel or King, while others left the most wonderful looking gifts. The young boy felt a growing desire to express his gratitude for these wonderful feelings, but his speech fled. So he continued kneeling content until late into the night in the warmth of this presence which he felt, but could not describe.

The thought came to him that this child was different than any that had ever been born. He felt that this child, whom they were calling Jesus, would do wonderful things for all people. He thought he must give the child something. A gift of some kind, but what did he have to give? Then he felt his chest and the ring. Haltingly, he crawled around the end of the stall for he did not want to disturb the atmosphere in the stable.

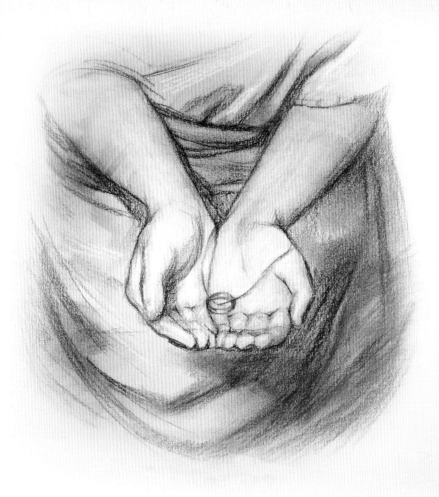

He reached into his tattered shirt and drew out the twine with the small silver ring and motioned to give it to the mother. Understanding the gesture, she nodded toward the newborn and smiled. Daniel stretched forth trembling hands and gently placed the twine around the infant's neck so that the ring lay softly against his small form.

His tears bathed the young King's feet as others would years later, but Daniel knew not the significance of the moment. The mother nodded acceptance with tears of her own, blessed the young boy, and held the baby and the ring close to her heart. For what remained of that night, Daniel slept a sleep of complete peace that he would know only one other time in his life.

The young boy grew. He continued to do what he could to build something positive of his dreadful state. However, his life did not improve nor did his fortune. Many times he fell into paths that were dark and dangerous, and there were events in his life that, when he thought of his mother and the feelings he had for that young family many years before, made him feel ashamed.

He survived somehow, living on the fringe of society until a day many years later when he was taken by the Romans and condemned as a thief. Admittedly, he looked the part for his clothes were torn and ragged, but he was accused wrongly and unjustly sentenced. There was little chance in those days for the truth to be heard from a man so poor. Destitute as he was, his defense fell upon deaf ears.

He walked carrying the very instrument of his punishment to that hill named Golgotha. There he was lashed to a wooden beam, lifted up, and left to suffer for his supposed crime, next to another taken for a similar offense. There were no crowds or mourners for the two condemned men. He was accustomed to such invisibility and endured it without complaint. During the first hour, a crowd gathered as a third man was led to the hill.

This man was different. He was beaten and battered yet his head was not bowed and his spirit unbroken. He was nailed to his cross, and the cries of his agony echoed in the hills. His robe was torn from him, and, as Daniel glanced at his tortured body, his eyes grew wide with wonder.

Around the third man's neck was revealed a very small silver ring held with a piece of twine. Daniel let out an involuntary cry as the ring was quickly ripped from the man's neck and pocketed by one of the centurion guards.

The third man turned his head slowly and glanced at Daniel. With eyes full of compassion, the man gave Daniel a look of recognition. The condemned man on the right interrupted the moment by shouting angrily at this man they called "King of the Jews." Daniel, with power he did not believe he still possessed, rebuked the man and said to the Lord, "Please, remember me when you come into your kingdom."

Jesus then spoke to Daniel saying, "Today, we shall be together in paradise." At that moment, he again felt a sweet peace that comforted his mind and heart as it had so many years before. Then his mind sensed these words, "Thank you, Daniel Ben-Yosef, for your faith has not wavered since long ago when you gave all you had to me; today I shall give you all that our Father hath in return."

Again, as before, he felt something special in the air. It was wonderful and familiar. In his waning conscious moments, he heard singing, and, within the chorus, his mother's voice rang out loud and strong. He felt the words, "It is finished," resound in his heart and somehow he knew something wonderful was beginning. As the lights in his mind went out, he prepared himself for this new beginning, for only then did he realize that because of this innocent man, now hanging lifeless beside him, he had always had hope. He had never been alone. Somewhere, they knew his name. There was a place prepared for him that night.

The Beginning